How does a
CLOUD
become a
THUNDERSTORM?

Mike Graf

www.raintreepublishers.co.uk
Visit our website to find out
more information about
Raintree books.

To order:
☎ Phone 0845 6044371
📄 Fax +44 (0) 1865 312263
💻 Email myorders@raintreepublishers.co.uk

Customers from outside the UK please telephone +44 1865 312262

Raintree is an imprint of Capstone Global Library Limited,
a company incorporated in England and Wales having its
registered office at 7 Pilgrim Street, London, EC4V 6LB
– Registered company number: 6695582

Edited by David Andrews and Laura Knowles
Designed by Richard Parker and Wagtail
Original illustrations © Capstone Global Library Ltd 2010
Illustrated by Jeff Edwards
Picture research by Mica Brancic
Originated by Modern Age Repro House Ltd
Printed and bound in China by CTPS

ISBN 978 1 406 21124 5 (hardback)
13 12 11 10 09
10 9 8 7 6 5 4 3 2 1

ISBN 978 1 406 21132 0 (paperback)
14 13 12 11 10
10 9 8 7 6 5 4 3 2 1

British Library Cataloguing in Publication Data
Graf, Mike
How does a cloud become a thunderstorm?. – (How does it
happen?)
551.5'54
A full catalogue record for this book is available from the
British Library.

Acknowledgements
We would like to thank the following for permission to
reproduce photographs: Photolibrary pp. **4** (Rainer Martini),
5 (Ken Redding), **6** (The Print Collector), **7** (Ron Watts), **9**
(Tom Chance), **10** (Adelina Sorani), **14** (Yoav Levy), **15**, **18**
(Imaging Imaging), **21** (Paul Katz), **21** (Walter Hodges), **24**
(Corbis -), **25** (Cicero Dias Viegas), **28** (Design Pics Inc),
istockphoto **background image** (© Dean Turner); Science
Photo Library pp. **23** (DANIEL L. OSBORNE), **26**, **27** (Jim
Reed Photography/Dean Schoeneck); Visuals Unlimited p. **16**
(© Inga Spence).

Cover photograph of a mixture of cumulus clouds and cirrus
clouds on a summer day (top) reproduced with permission
of Photolibrary/Photdisc/Kyu Oh, and lightning (bottom)
reproduced with permission of Photolibrary/Flirt Collection/
Robert Matheson.

Every effort has been made to contact copyright holders of
any material reproduced in this book. Any omissions will
be rectified in subsequent printings if notice is given to the
publisher.

Disclaimer
All the Internet addresses (URLs) given in this book were valid
at the time of going to press. However, due to the dynamic
nature of the Internet, some addresses may have changed, or
sites may have changed or ceased to exist since publication.
While the author and Publishers regret any inconvenience this
may cause readers, no responsibility for any such changes can
be accepted by either the author or the Publishers.

Contents

A brewing storm 4

Thunderstorms in the past 6

A moist beginning 8

A cloud is born 10

The types of cloud 12

Clouds and storms 14

What is a thunderstorm? 16

What causes lightning? 18

Where lightning strikes 20

Many types of lightning 22

A clap of thunder 24

Lightning safety 26

The water cycle 28

Glossary 30

Find out more 31

Index 32

Some words are shown in bold, **like this**. You can find out what they mean by looking in the glossary.

A brewing storm

It is mid-afternoon on a summer day. High up in the **atmosphere**, white, wispy clouds drift by. But, in the distance, darker clouds loom. These grey clouds approach slowly. As they approach, a rumbling can be heard in the distance.

Approaching cumulus clouds mean rain might be coming soon.

Soon the dark clouds are overhead. A sprinkling of rain hits the ground. A flash of **lightning** streaks across the sky, followed by a roar of **thunder**. Now the rain is beating the ground.

These campers have been caught in a sudden downpour.

Where did this thunderstorm come from? It began as invisible moisture that rose up from the ground. This water **vapour** gathered to form a cloud. Finally there was too much water for the cloud to hold, and rain began to fall. The rising and sinking air, combined with the droplets of water bumping into each other, created electrical **charges**, meaning positive or negative properties. The electrical charges hit the ground in the form of lightning. The once-harmless cloud had turned into a dangerous thunderstorm.

Rumbling across Earth

There are about 1,800 thunderstorms each day that hit the planet. Lightning strikes Earth about 100 times a second, and 20 million times in a year.

Thunderstorms in the past

Thunderstorms have amazed people for a long time. Some people thought thunderstorms were the gods' way of punishing them. The ancient Greeks believed **lightning** was a weapon used by gods. They even built temples (places of worship) on areas that had been hit by lightning. They did this because they thought the ground struck was sacred, or holy.

In this image, the god Thor is getting ready to throw his hammer.

Thor

Viking myths (stories) spoke of a god of **thunder** and lightning called Thor. Thor was said to sometimes throw a hammer at his enemies. The hammer whirling through the sky created lightning. The thunder was Thor's chariot whisking across the sky.

Some ancient cultures believed lightning was created by bad spirits. Many villages kept church bells ringing to scare these evil spirits away and to keep lightning strikes from hitting them.

The Thunderbird is often carved on the top of Native American totem poles.

The Thunderbird

Some Native Americans believed lightning was made by the colourful feathers of a bird called the Thunderbird. They believed that thunder was made when the bird flapped its wings.

A moist beginning

Clouds often begin with sunshine. The Sun's rays heat the water on the surface of a lake, sea, or even water contained within land, causing it to **evaporate**. It becomes water **vapour**, which is a gas made of invisible droplets of water in the air. This vapour rises from the water, adding moisture to the warm air that has been heated by the Sun.

When water is warmed by the Sun, water vapour rises into the air. As the vapour cools, clouds are formed.

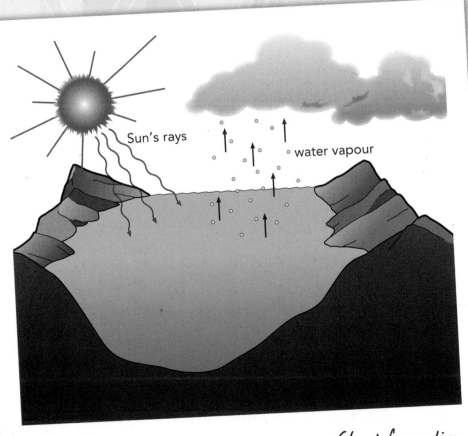

Sun's rays

water vapour

Cloud formation

This warm, moist air rises higher because it weighs less than the cooler air. Eventually it reaches a higher level of the **atmosphere**, where the air is cold.

The water vapour can bump into **particles** (small pieces) of dust or smoke in the air. These particles might occur naturally, or they may result from **pollution**. Pollution happens when chemicals get into the air, soil, and water. These conditions can cause the water vapour to become visible again. The **dew point** is the temperature that air needs to reach to be cool enough to turn water vapour into a liquid again.

Dew droplets

Morning dew

The dew that forms some mornings is water vapour that has cooled enough to become a liquid. Dew forms at night or in the early morning because temperatures are cooler then.

A cloud Is born

Thousands of water droplets can cling to dust **particles** or each other in the air. They gather together as **condensation**, which is visible water in the air. This starts forming a cloud.

Under certain conditions, the cloud can get larger and larger. Eventually the cloud might become saturated (full of water). When the cloud becomes full, it releases **precipitation**. Precipitation is water falling as rain, hail, sleet, or snow.

Snow is one of the four main types of precipitation.

Clouds are typically white at the top and grey near the bottom. The Sun lights up the top of the cloud. The bottom of the cloud is blocked or shaded from direct light, making it a darker colour. Thunderclouds are very dark at their base. This is because they are so thick that little light can get through to their bottom.

Water vapour from planes can turn into clouds called contrails.

Aeroplane clouds

As aeroplanes fly overhead, they leave a trail of water vapour and smoke. Water vapour can cling to the smoke particles, forming droplets. This leaves a cloud behind called a contrail.

The types of cloud

Clouds come in many shapes and sizes. It depends on many factors: how much water the clouds contain, how high they are, and how much wind is in the air.

Stratus and cumulus cloud heights

Cumulus clouds often look like puffy wisps of cotton. These are the clouds that come in many shapes – they might look like an object or an animal. The bottoms of these clouds are found less than 2,000 metres (6,500 feet) off the ground.

Stratus clouds are also low to the ground. Fog is a kind of stratus cloud that clings to the ground. Places near the sea often get fog as do cold valleys on winter mornings.

Cirrus clouds are so thin that you can see through them. These clouds form more than 6,000 metres (19,500 feet) up in the air. They are typically made of ice **crystals**, which are patterns of ice.

Cumulonimbus clouds are tall and thick. They form when cumulus clouds gather together. Cumulonimbus clouds often end up as thunderstorms.

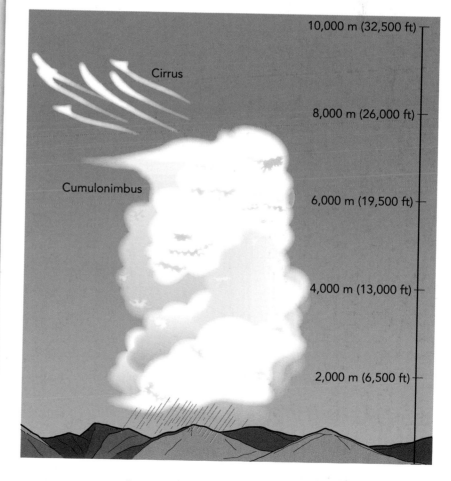

Cirrus and Cumulonimbus cloud heights

Clouds and storms

How can you predict when a storm cloud will form? Sometimes you can predict by measuring the **air pressure**, which is the density (weight) of the air.

Under pressure

You can measure air pressure by reading an instrument called a **barometer**. The level of mercury (a silver-white metal) in the barometer rises and lowers as the pressure changes. A reading of 760 millimetres (30 inches) is about average. A lower reading may mean a storm is brewing!

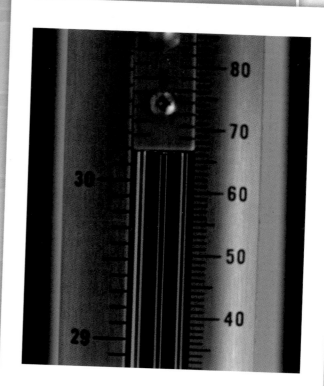

A barometer measures air pressure

Higher air pressure means that the air is thicker and heavier. This air is usually too heavy to rise, so big clouds are less likely to form. Clear weather is often the result.

Lower air pressure means that the air is lighter. This air is more likely to rise, bringing more moisture up into the clouds. The result can be thick, heavy **cumulonimbus clouds** – the type that bring storms.

Satellite image of storm clouds over Florida, USA

Hurricanes, which have large cumulonimbus clouds within them, can bring very severe weather.

Often a storm will form near where warm air meets colder air. This is called a cold front. The warm air rises over the colder air. As it rises, it cools and **condenses** (changes from gas or vapour to liquid) into a mass of storm clouds.

What is a thunderstorm?

The clouds that create thunderstorms are very tall. They are full of unstable air. In some places, these clouds can grow to over 15,000 metres (50,000 feet) tall – higher than Mount Everest! When clouds are this high, the air at the top of the cloud is much colder than the air at the bottom. This causes the air in the cloud to move around.

The nozzles on this plane spray silver iodide

Bringing more rain

Scientists have found a way to enhance storms in areas that need more rain. When storms come through, aeroplanes spray a cold chemical called silver iodide into the clouds. It cools the cloud, causing the moisture to **condense** and rain to fall.

As water droplets and hail within a thunder cloud grow, they get so heavy that the rising air cannot hold them. Then the clouds begin to release rain or hail. This cycle can happen over and over.

Finally, the falling rain or hail cuts off the rising **currents**, which are movements of large areas of air. The storm stops collecting moist air. If this continues, the thunderstorm calms down. Most thunderstorms only last about 30 minutes.

Thunderstorms develop in stages, from growing (top), to mature (middle), to dissipating (bottom).

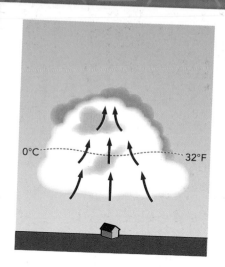
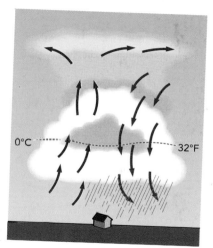
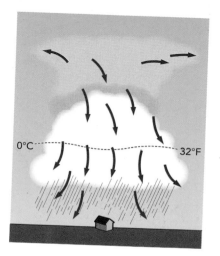

The cycle of a storm cloud

What causes lightning?

Scientists are still learning about the causes of **lightning**. What they do know is that it starts from electrical **charges** in a storm cloud.

High up in a storm cloud, bits of ice bump into each other as they move. Some scientists believe that as they collide, some **particles** become positively charged. Others become negatively charged. The particles with heavier, negative charges may collect at the bottom of the cloud. The particles with lighter, positive charges rise.

These dark storm clouds could bring flashes of lightning.

Negative charges in a storm cloud attract positive charges on the ground.

In nature, opposite charges attract. So, underneath the negative charges at the bottom of a storm cloud, positive charges collect. Finally, the attraction becomes too great. A positive charge from the ground reaches up to a negative charge extending down from the cloud. When they connect, their path is a bolt of lightning.

Where lightning strikes

Not all **lightning** strikes the ground. Sometimes lightning bolts flash inside a cloud. The negative **charges** in one part of the cloud reach out to the positive charges in another part. This is called an intracloud flash.

Other lightning bolts seem to come out of nowhere. These are "bolts from the blue". They come from the side of a storm cloud that is many kilometres away.

Lightning coming from clouds can go in various directions.

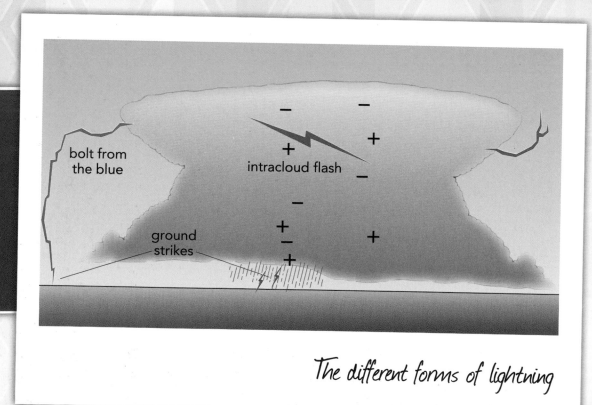

bolt from the blue

intracloud flash

ground strikes

The different forms of lightning

When lightning strikes the ground, it is more likely to hit tall objects such as trees and poles. Many trees that have been hit have lightning scars. Lightning can also strike the roof of a house.

Tall objects such as buildings are more likely to be struck by lightning than objects closer to the ground.

Lightning rods

When a house is hit, lightning can travel through the home's electrical system. This can be dangerous. Some buildings have metal poles called lightning rods to attract lightning. This helps protect the structure by leading the electricity into the ground.

Many types of lightning

Lightning bolts can be more than 90 kilometres (60 miles) long. Each strike is different. Sheet lightning happens in a cloud. Because of the lightning's location, the whole cloud looks like a white sheet. Ribbon lightning's side streaks make it look like a ribbon.

This forked lightning bolt is spreading out sideways across the sky.

Strange lightning

Lightning can look like a string of beads for a brief moment after a strike. Sometimes circular shapes are connected to a lightning strike. These glowing balls are called ball lightning.

Lightning above a cloud – called sprites – are often red or orange in colour.

Dry lightning occurs when there is a lightning storm, but no **precipitation**. Sprites are lightning strikes that happen above the thunderstorm. They can be reddish orange or greenish blue. These are also sometimes seen as blue jets of lightning.

A clap of thunder

When **lightning** strikes, it sends off not just light, but also sound – **thunder**. What causes thunder? When a lightning bolt hits an area, the air temperature and **air pressure** suddenly increase. This rapidly expanding air makes a shock wave. The wave ripples out in all directions, like a pebble dropping in a pond. When the wave hits your ear, it produces the sound of thunder.

Sound waves act in the same way as the ripples in this water.

Lightning and thunder always happen at the same time. But light travels faster than sound. This means that we see the lightning before we hear the thunder. If thunder is heard very soon after a flash of lightning, the lightning is very close. When a lightning bolt hits nearby, thunder sounds like a very large clap. If it is far away, it might sound more like rumbling.

Storm clouds are gathering. Will there be lightning soon?

From flash to bang

People can estimate the distance of the lightning by counting the time between the flash of lightning and the sound of thunder. A five-second count means lightning is about 1.6 kilometres (1 mile) away. This is called the flash-to-bang method. If you hear thunder 30 seconds or less after seeing lightning, head for cover. You could be in danger.

Lightning safety

The most important thing to do during a thunderstorm is to stay inside.

Indoor safety

Here are some ways to stay safe indoors:

- Stay away from any electrical items and sockets.
- Stay away from windows and doors.

Franklin's dangerous experiment

Don't follow Franklin

In a famous weather experiment, US statesman and inventor Benjamin Franklin was said to have flown a kite into a thunderstorm in 1752. When he did this he saw electricity jump from a key on a kite string onto his hand close by. Don't repeat this experiment, however – he could have been **electrocuted**!

Lightning is not the only dangerous force of nature. A tornado can also be very destructive.

Outdoor safety

If for some reason you cannot get indoors, there are steps that can make you safer outside:

- If **lightning** is very close, squat down, get on your tiptoes, and bend forwards in a crouched position. This makes you smaller and allows as little of your body as possible to touch the ground.

- Get away from any tall objects.
- Stay off hills, mountains, and open fields. Get to a lower area.
- Spread out if you are in a group of people.
- Stay away from water or metal.
- If you are outside during a storm and your hair starts to rise, your skin tingles, or you hear a humming sound, this is extremely dangerous. Lightning may be about to strike nearby.

The water cycle

Storms bring **precipitation** to Earth. This is part of the **water cycle**. In Earth's water cycle, water is always going between Earth and the **atmosphere**, the layer of gases and air that surrounds Earth.

Snow brings melting water to streams, which is a part of the water cycle.

The water cycle starts by rain or snow falling on oceans or lakes. Then, as the sun warms that water, it **evaporates** into the air as a **vapour**.

The water vapour rises into the atmosphere. There it will meet cooler air. **Condensation** occurs with the cooler air and smoke or dust. The water droplets eventually grow too heavy to stay in the air and fall as precipitation.

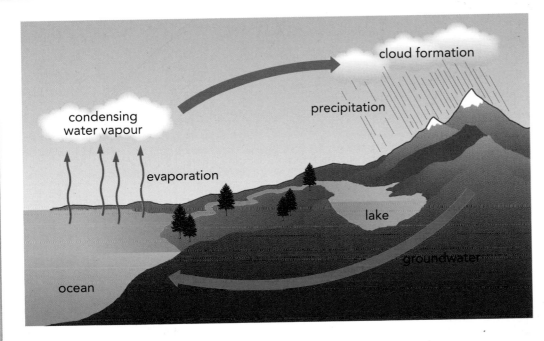

The water cycle

The water cycle is Earth's way of staying well-watered.

Everlasting water

The water we drink was also drunk by dinosaurs millions of years ago. There is no new water on Earth. It is always being recycled by the water cycle.

Glossary

air pressure density (weight) of the air

atmosphere layer of gases and air that surrounds Earth

barometer instrument for measuring the pressure or weight of the air

charge positive or negative electrical properties found in a particle

cirrus cloud cloud high in the atmosphere that is thin and wispy and made of ice crystals

condensation process of changing from gas or vapour to a liquid

condense change from a gas or vapour to a liquid

crystal solid substance made up of tiny parts arranged in an ordered, repeating pattern. Ice sometimes forms as crystals.

cumulonimbus cloud large, potentially dangerous cloud associated with thunderstorms

cumulus cloud puffy cloud that looks like cotton

current movement of a large area of air or water

dew point temperature at which water vapour condenses into liquid water

electrocute when someone is injured or killed by an electric shock

evaporate turn from a liquid into a gas

lightning large electrical charges or impulses in the atmosphere

particle extremely small piece or amount of something

pollution when human-made chemicals get into the air, soil, or water

precipitation water falling from clouds as rain, hail, snow, or sleet

stratus cloud low-level cloud close to the ground, such as fog

thunder sound that follows lightning and is caused by rapidly expanding air

vapour gas formed by water evaporating (disappearing) into the air

water cycle constant recycling of water from Earth to the atmosphere and back

Find out more

Books

Do you still have questions about clouds and thunderstorms? There is much more to learn about these fascinating topics. You can find out more by picking up some of these books from your local library:

The Earth's Weather (Earth's Processes), Rebecca Harman (Heinemann Library, 2006)

Weird Weather, Andy Horsley (Ticktock, 2006)

Wild Weather, Blakes (A & C Black, 2007)

Websites

Try some of the experiments on this site:
www.metoffice.gov.uk/education/kids/weather_experiments. html

Have a look at the fun animations on this site:
www.bbc.co.uk/schools/whatisweather

For more information on thunderstorms and other weather dangers, go to this website:
http://eo.ucar.edu/webweather

Index

aeroplanes 11, 16
air currents 17
air pressure 14, 15, 24
ancient beliefs 6–7
atmosphere 4, 9, 28, 29

ball lightning 23
barometer 14

cirrus clouds 13
clouds 4, 5, 8, 10, 11, 12–13, 14, 15, 16, 17, 19, 25
cold front 15
condensation 10, 15, 16, 29
contrails 11
cumulonimbus clouds 13, 15
cumulus clouds 4, 12

dew 9
dew point 9
dry lightning 23
dust and smoke particles 9, 10

electrical charges 5, 18, 19, 20

electricity 21, 26
evaporation 8, 28
evil spirits 7

flash-to-bang method 25
fog 13
forked lightning 22
Franklin, Benjamin 26

gods of thunder and lightning 6
Greeks, ancient 6

hail 10, 17
hurricanes 15, 26

ice 13, 18
intracloud flashes 20

lightning 4, 5, 6, 7, 18, 19, 20–23, 24, 25, 27
lightning rods 21
lightning scars 21

Native Americans 7

pollution 9
positive and negative charges 5, 18, 19, 20

precipitation 10, 23, 28, 29
predicting storms 14

rain 4, 10, 16, 17, 28
ribbon lightning 22

safety 26–27
sheet lightning 22
shock waves 24
silver iodide 16
sleet 10
snow 10, 28
sprites 23
storm clouds 11, 13, 14, 15, 16, 17, 18, 19, 25
stratus clouds 12, 13

Thor 6
thunder 4, 24–25
Thunderbird 7
tornadoes 26, 27

Viking myths 6

water cycle 28–29
water droplets 5, 8, 10, 17, 29
water vapour 5, 8, 9, 11, 28, 29